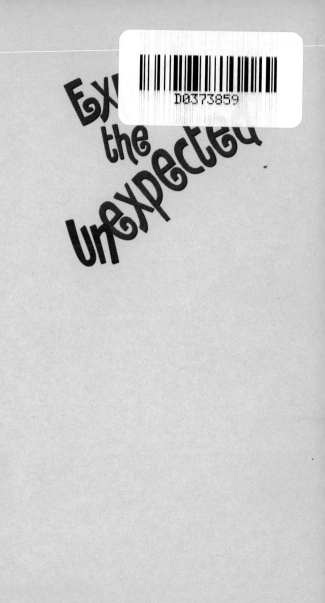

Expect
the
Unexpected

Also by Robynn Clairday:

Tell me This Isn t Happening!

Collected by Robynn Clairday

SCHOLASTIC INC.
New York Toronto London Auckland Sydney
Mexico City New Delhi Hong Kong

No part of this publication may be reproduced in whole or in part,
or stored in a retrieval system or transmitted in any form or by
any means, electronic, mechanical, photocopying, recording, or
otherwise, without written permission of the publisher. For infor-
mation regarding permission, write to Scholastic Inc., Attention:
Permissions Dept., 555 Broadway, New York, NY 10012.

ISBN 0-439-21581-1

12 11 10 9 8 7 6 5 4 3 2 1   0 1 2 3 4 5/0

Printed in the U.S.A.   01
First Scholastic printing, October 2000

Table of Contents

Acknowledgments

First, I'd like to thank all of the fantastic kids who contributed their stories and who made this book possible. Thanks also to my "angels," Helene, Kristin, Bessie, and Suzanne. I am especially appreciative of the help I received from Holly Lebed, Nick Nestoros, Sharron Thurmond, Shan Tabor, Marsha L. Smith, Dennis Sampier, Jean Thompson, and Neda Kia. Thanks to Shatha from the Young Girl Writers Club and to Melisa from Girl Zone.

Melvin Hazel, Connie Cox, Sam Farmer, Shawn Gist, Ms. Gist, Angela Goode, Sean Davan, Walter Bibb, Viv Swoboda, Karen Kernaghan, Penny Matos, and Brumilda Irizarry all have to be recognized for their unbelievably generous assistance.

Of course, I can't forget the ladies of the OTB club, Kari Cimbalik and Michelle Milton and to the honorary member, Ronnie. Their friendship and support are priceless. I am also grateful for my wonderful cyber-crew: Michelle Churchman, Glynne Gilmore, Cathy Krusberg, Sara Nguyen, and David Bradley.

Thanks to my shining lights, Julie and Em.

A big thanks to the celebrities in this book, who were kind enough to offer their own stories. As always, my family and dear friends deserve my gratitude for their loyalty and love. And I can't thank my terrific editor, Kate, enough for being so, well, terrific.

And last but not least, thanks to Matt, who's more super than any superhero.

Expect the Unexpected

You guys made me do it. You really did. When I finished my last book, *Tell Me This Isn't Happening*, I thought I'd heard the last of super-embarrassing stories. I kidded about doing a sequel, but I really thought it was over. We were all going to live free of humiliation from then on, right?

Wrong. In the meantime, you guys were getting yourselves into such mortifying situations that, well, we couldn't ignore what was going on. It was an embarrassment epidemic! The stories came from all over the country, from Puerto Rico to Oklahoma and Massachusetts — even Hollywood. They were so cringe-worthy that we decided we had to do the sequel after all. It would have been a crime not to.

These kids told their stories in their very own

1

words, but only after I promised to change their names. When you read further, you'll definitely see why. You may even be thinking, "Hey, wait a minute, this happened to me — how did she know?"

I didn't. The secret is we all have something in common. We all get embarrassed at least once in our lives. And probably a lot more times than that.

But before we go on, I have to be fair and confess a story of my own.

I went to a restaurant with friends and family one evening. Afterward we decided to go shopping. We were wandering up and down the sidewalk when my friend grabbed me and hissed, "Your pants. Come with me." Mystified, I followed her into a nearby bathroom. She pushed me in front of the mirror and told me to look behind me. I did — and let out a yelp. I had sat in brown gravy and was walking all over the place with it on me! Let's put it this way — no one could have missed it. Too bad I was walking behind my friends for a good thirty minutes; otherwise they could have clued me in sooner.

To top it off, I was wearing white pants.

'Nuff said. You get the picture. But, seriously,

that's the way it goes. Life is always waiting to spring something embarrassing on us, no matter how cool we are or how hard we try to avoid disasters. I can't guarantee it, of course, but one way you *might* stay out of trouble is by reading this book.

Chapter One

Titanic

Maybe you've seen the movie, or maybe you just heard about it. It's about a ship that sinks, but more important it's about two people, Jack and Rose, whose romance just doesn't work out. It's amazing how many things go wrong when your crush — or even your maybe-crush — is around! Somehow, when the opposite sex is nearby, you're most likely to find yourself in a disaster movie of your own.

Hot Lips

I was at a friend's birthday party. After a while, we decided to play spin the bottle. It was my turn to spin and when the bottle stopped, it pointed right at my crush. I was so nervous that when I stepped toward him, I tripped over the glass bottle. Instead of kissing *him*, I kissed his shoe!

— Jonelle

Titanic 2

Once I went swimming with my mom, and there were a lot of people there. One cute boy, named EJ, was floating in the pool on a tube. He was coming right toward me. Then, suddenly, the tube was pushing me against the side of the pool. Afterward, everyone was looking at me, and I realized why. I'd cut my lip on the hard edge of the swimming pool, and there was blood everywhere! I could tell EJ was embarrassed. And so was I.

My mom wrapped me in a towel and put another towel on my lip to put pressure on it. We went home and I put an ice pack on my mouth. My brand-new suit had blood all over it. Then I decided to take a nap. When I woke up, I saw that my bathing suit was see-through when it was wet. That is the first and last time I wore that suit! I didn't want to show my face outside of the house again.

— Antonia

Titanic 3 — Another Water Trauma

When I was about nine, my sister and I were walking to the pool with her friends. That's when it all began.

On the way to the pool, one of her friends threw his sandal at me. I started to chase him but I tripped and fell. All the way to the pool, he kept saying, "Maddie's trippin'" over and over.

Then, at the pool, something even worse happened. I was getting ready to go off the high diving board, and my boyfriend was right behind me. I jumped and as I hit the water, my bathing top came all the way up! I was totally exposed. The next day, my boyfriend told everyone at school, and I was the laugh of the day.

— Maddie

Falling for You

I'd just learned how to ride a bike, and my friend Sela had been helping me learn. I'd been practicing on her bike. I'd just found out that I rode pretty poorly on sidewalks, so I decided to go on the grass. I tried going fast.

There were a lot of trees in front of me. I turned the bike and was lucky I didn't hit any. I was weaving my bike every which way to avoid the trees.

When I finally got past them, I sped up fast, but somehow my shoelace caught onto the bike chain! I tried to get it loose but I crashed. I felt so embarrassed. There was nothing else to do but close my eyes and pretend to faint!

— Diego

Geronimo!

One day, I went to my best friend Tisha's house. We were playing basketball, but then Tisha dared me to kiss my boyfriend, so he and I went into the garage. Right when he kissed me on the cheek, Tisha's little sister came running in! My boyfriend was so startled that he ran down the street and jumped into a ditch. We were so embarrassed.

No one else knows about this. But my boyfriend and I aren't together anymore. Now we are just friends.

— Shania

I Love You, You Love Me . . .

I had a basketball game, and we were playing the best kids in the league. I got dressed, but I didn't have that many clothes to choose from, because they were getting washed. So I had to put on a T-shirt and short shorts.

The game started, and I was taking the ball down to shoot it. I looked at the sidelines, and my mom was mouthing something that I couldn't understand. I shot the ball and made a basket. Our team played really well.

Near the end of the game, though, I started to feel cold. And all of a sudden, the cutest boy I'd ever seen walked up to me and said, "Excuse me, but your panties are showing."

I turned bright red. My short shorts had ridden all the way up. It wouldn't have been *that* bad, except that I was wearing Barney underwear! And for a nine-year-old, that's bad.

— Maia

Lost in Love

One day, I was shopping at Wal-Mart with my mom. Suddenly, I spotted this cute boy. He was a total hottie. I stared at him for about three minutes and didn't pay attention to where I was walking. The next thing I knew I'd crashed right into a pole!

— Shay

Head over Heels

I was in music class when it happened. We were about to line up to leave, and I was standing at the bottom of the riser. I leaned against it and for some reason lost my balance. What's worse is I fell right on the cutest guy in the school, Brandon McCartney! We collapsed to the floor together, and the entire class laughed at me. They called me "Big Bird" because I looked so clumsy. Next time, I'll wait for Brandon to get off the riser before I even move!

— Robin

Never Again!

It was the day before Halloween, and my crush had invited me to his party. I was dressed up as Britney Spears, wearing a blue tube top and jeans.

Everyone was allowed to pick a song and dance to it. I chose "You Drive Me Crazy." I was dancing when my top slid down, right in front of all the guys, including my crush. They stared at me, but no one said anything. I managed to pull my top up quickly. Then this other really cute guy started laughing!

I'll never wear anything like that again — at least not in public!

— Julianna

Celebrity Confession: Michelle Krusiec, who plays Sui, on NBC's <u>One World</u>

I was in the fifth grade, and we were doing math problems at the chalkboard. On this particular day, I had chosen to wear one of those one-piece jumpers to school. It was lavender and corduroy (which was very cool at the time) but the jumper kept making my underwear ride up my butt. And since it was a one-piece outfit, there was no way of fixing my wedgie discreetly!

Since everyone, including the teacher, was at the chalkboard and facing in the same direction, I decided now was the moment to relieve my very uncomfortable situation. I crept my hand back there and tried to fix the problem, when I heard a burst of laughter from behind me. I looked to the doorway and saw one of my classmates, who had just returned from the rest room, doubled over in laughter. She was practically in tears, and I was so embarrassed because she had caught me in "mid-pick." I just stammered and said, "What? What?" as if nothing had happened. But to this day, I will never pick wedgies in public.

Kari Cimbalik, editor of the _Take Good Care of Me_ parenting book series (Sourcebooks 1999, 2000)

When I was in middle school, I had a huge crush on this one guy. It was lunchtime, and people were in a line all the way down the staircase, since our cafeteria happened to be in the basement. I was at the top of the stairs when I spotted my crush several steps below me. I was craning my neck to see him when I stepped forward, forgetting where I was. Suddenly, I tumbled down the entire flight of stairs, and everyone was staring at me! My hands and knees were all scraped up, but worse I felt like a fool.

Everyone was asking if I was okay, but I just wanted to pretend like it had never happened. My crush must have seen me fall, but he didn't say a word or look my way. I'd just made an idiot of myself, and he acted as if I didn't exist!

Chapter Two

The Y-Files

Sometimes the biggest mysteries aren't about aliens but about us humans. Shouldn't we call them *The Y-Files*? After all, we want to know *why* we get into so much trouble. *Why* do the craziest things happen to us? *Why* don't we always know what's going on? *Why* do people and things trip us up so often?

Clothes Encounter

It was a cold fall day, and I had nothing clean to wear except my Power Ranger pjs. I thought they looked okay and that maybe no one would notice they were pajamas.

But when I walked into class, everyone started laughing. I turned around and saw that part of my pjs had gotten caught on the doorknob and ripped! I wanted to run home, but I had to stay at school for the whole day. After that, I quit wearing pjs anywhere but to bed!

— Reilly

Bunny Boo-boo

We were at music class, but before we did anything else, we always played a game called, "Who Has the Bunny?" In this game, there were two stuffed rabbits that you passed around the circle of people, and if one landed on you then you had to sing, "I have the bunny." Then two people in the middle of the circle, who had their eyes closed, had to guess who had the bunny.

Neither of the rabbits had landed on me yet for some reason, I still sang out loud that I had one. Everyone was staring at me! And they all started laughing. My mom still teases me about it.

— Denise

Telling Tales

I was sitting in my room when my mom came in and told me that my sister had lost the remote. She asked me to help her look for it. So, I looked under the table, and found it right away. I shouted "Here it is!" so everyone would know.

I picked it up and jumped in surprise. I had just grabbed my black cat's tail by mistake! She meowed and ran away. I didn't think anything of it, but my mom and sister did. They laughed their heads off.

I was even more embarrassed when my mom told everybody about it. They all kept asking if I really thought the cat's tail was the remote. I said yes, because the remote was black and so was my cat's tail.

— Dakota

Red-faced and Red-handed

I once drew a cut on my hand with a red marker. I thought my teacher was going to believe it was a real scrape, and maybe give me a Band-

Aid. When I showed it to her, she said, "Do you want me to take you to the doctor's?" She was teasing me, and everybody heard. I was so embarrassed.

— Albert

Funny Bone

My most embarrassing moment happened when I was in kindergarten. My teacher asked me in Spanish to show my elbow to her. In Spanish, an elbow is "codo." I thought she was saying "coro," which means chorus in English. I believed that she wanted me to sing like I was in a chorus. So I started singing! Everyone in my class started laughing, and I realized my mistake.

— Anya

Finger-licking Good

Once I was eating fried chicken in a Church's restaurant, when suddenly a piece of chicken fell from my hands. Since I was so hungry, I picked it up from the floor and ate it anyway. Then I looked around. Everybody in the restaurant was staring in amazement at me, and I felt so embarrassed that I threw the rest of my meal in the trash.

— Hector

Water Whammy

I was five years old and went to a public swimming pool, because my day care had decided to take all of us kids there to play. I didn't know how to swim, and I was scared of drowning.

When we first got there, I stood staring down at the water, minding my own business. Then along came this girl named Ashton, who pushed me in for no good reason. Splash! I was lucky that the water was only three feet high.

I climbed out of the pool and went looking for Ashton. I walked down to the deeper end when somebody pushed me in again! Splash! I don't know who it was, but I'm guessing it was Ashton again. This time the water was four feet deep. Trying to swim — and thinking I was drowning — I saw two boys sitting on the edge of the pool. I tried to climb out of the pool by grabbing on to one of the boys, but I accidentally pulled on his swimming trunks. I nearly pulled them all the way off!

Finally, the boys and my cousin came in to help me. I couldn't move, because I was embarrassed for the *third* time that day. I still don't know how to swim.

— Eileen

Turtle Dance

One day when I was in school, our teacher told us to get our math books out. I bent down and reached for my book, which was in my backpack on the floor. When I yanked it out, the entire desk tumbled over and fell on top of me! I was wriggling around and couldn't get out from under it. The entire class started laughing, and I was so embarrassed. Finally, I was able to free myself and get up.

My teacher said it reminded him of the commercial that says, "Help, I've fallen and I can't get up." Everyone started laughing again. They still bring it up every once in a while.

— Jenny

Nowhere to Go

One day, my cousin, my sister, and I walked to our church. We were very well dressed and elegant. When we were halfway there, though, a neighbor told us that there was no Mass in the afternoon that Sunday! To hide our mistake, we told her that we were going to visit my uncle, who happened to live in the same neighborhood as the church. Then, to keep up with our story, we had to go to my uncle's house. Once we got there, we found he wasn't even home. So we were embarrassed twice — but the second time was our own fault.

— Daniella

Ladies First

When I was eight years old, I went to a skating rink. After skating a while, I got tired and decided to sit down and have a drink. I started skating again when, all of a sudden, I had to go to the rest room. I skated as fast as I could to the exit, then went to find it.

I went inside, and that's when I noticed that I was in the boys' bathroom! Even more embarrassing, there were boys in there! When I rushed back out, a lady came over and pointed at the bathroom sign that said "Men."

— Deena

Teddy Bear — Where?

One morning, my family was rushing around getting ready for school. I put on my pink teddy bear T-shirt. It was my favorite! Then I went to school. I was doing a lot of work and was very busy. All of a sudden, my teacher, Ms. Milton, looked at me funny. She then came over and whispered in my ear.

I was wearing my shirt backward! My friend Tim and I laughed really hard, but I felt silly.

— Melinda

Hello?

I was walking home from school and came to a noisy intersection. I pushed the WALK button, so that I could cross the street. I waited a bit. I was thinking of something else and looking in another direction, so I didn't realize that the WALK signal had finally come on. Then all of these cars that were waiting to pass started beeping at me! I was just standing there. Next time, I'll pay attention.

— Carter

Aisle Be Looking for You

I was in Wal-Mart with my mom, and we were shopping in the medicine section. I was trying to talk her into buying me a Power Ranger. I was five years old at the time.

"Tell me more about this Power Ranger," my mom said.

I tried explaining how Nitro got his name and how the Power Rangers got started. I was so into it that I was closing my eyes while I was talking. When I opened them, I was alone, and my mom was nowhere to be seen. I started crying!

Then this blond lady, who had a voice like a man's, said, "Hey, your mom's right over there."

She pointed to the next aisle, and there was

my mom! I was so embarrassed, because everyone was watching.

— Brian

Celebrity Confession: Ashley Monique Clark, who plays Sydney on ABC's <u>The Hughleys</u>

One time I was in New York City, and I was staying in a fancy skyscraper hotel. My room was on one of the highest floors, and I decided to look out the window to check out the spectacular view. But the window only opened halfway, so when I went to pull my head back in, I got stuck in the window! It took a while, but I finally twisted the right way and freed myself. I'm sure it was funny to see me from down on the street.

Chapter Three

Field of Dreams

In the movie *Field of Dreams* all the people wanted to do was to play baseball. And we can relate. Whether it's soccer, football, gymnastics, or whatever, sports can be really important, and we just want to do our best. But, stuff happens! We want to win that big game, but sometimes surviving the embarrassment *is* all that we can do.

Hanging Around

Six years old, big game, goalpost. These are all the words it takes to describe what happened. It was a pretty nice day, but not for our soccer team. We were trailing 7–0. It was terrible. And to make it even more miserable, it was my turn to be the goalie.

While wandering around the goal area, a kid from the other team dared me to climb to the top of the goalpost. There were two choices, the right one and the one I took. Soon I was hanging from my knees and too scared to get down.

"Hello, can anybody hear me out there? I'm hanging from a goalpost!" I yelled.

Nobody, not even my coach, saw me. The best thing my mom could do was videotape me. Soon everybody was laughing at me, hanging upside down from the post with a bright red face.

— Darren

Doing the Splits

One summer day, my mom dropped me off at gymnastics practice. Since it was so hot outside, I had to wear shorts even if they had holes in them. I started practicing, and my teacher's sister and friends were watching.

After my friend did her routine, it was my turn and everyone watched me do a handstand flip.

Suddenly, I knew something was wrong. When I looked down, I saw that the holes in my shorts had torn all the way up to my waist! I was so embarrassed.

— Angelique

Batter Up

It was my turn up at bat, and there were two outs in the last inning. Our teams were tied. The first pitch came zooming down the plate, and the umpire shouted, "Strike!"

The next pitch came zooming outside. The umpire yelled, "Ball." Then another one just like it.

The third ball. Another pitch came right down the plate, and I swung. The umpire called another strike. I hit again, and it was a ball again!

Now I was starting to shake as I stepped out of the batter's box. I kept thinking about how this was the last inning and how we were tied. And now, there were two strikes and three balls. Finally, I was able to concentrate and stepped back into the batter's box.

The last ball came right down the heart of the plate. I swung as hard as I could and heard a big cracking noise. Had I hit a home run? No! I had hit the catcher's helmet. Luckily, he wasn't hurt!

— Duncan

Let Go!

I was in a basketball game and was going to pass the ball. I did a three-sixty pass but I forgot to let go of it! My coach took me out of the game. As I walked off the court, all of my friends were watching me. I was laughing and crying at the same time.

— Jed

Let 'Er Rip

When I was ten years old, I called my friends to talk about playing football. We ended up going to the field and picked teams. It was Ned, Vinnie, and me against Mac, Declin, and BJ. Soon, the other team was winning by seven points.

Then Ned threw the ball to me, and I caught it. I made a touchdown. We went for a two-point conversion and I made that, too. Instead of cheering, though, my team was laughing. I wondered why. Then Declin told me that I had a big hole in the back of my pants!

— Tyler

Strike Three — Not!

It was my fifth game of the baseball season. It was the third inning, I had walked three times and I had hit the ball five times. I had also made one out.

My mom, dad, and brother were sitting in the van watching the game, because it was cold and windy outside.

The announcer said, "Next up to bat, Kyla."

I grabbed the bat and walked up to the plate. The ball was pitched four times, and I had two strikes and two balls. The last ball was pitched too low, right below my knees, and I knew not to swing at it.

But the referee said it was strike three, and that I was out! I walked back to the dugout with my head down. I knew it was a wrong call.

Then my dad leaned out of the van window

and called out, "How short do you think she is? That ball was too low. That was no strike."

He was right. But I was so embarrassed. I kept my eyes away from our van while the girls on my team kept looking around trying to figure out who had spoken.

— Kyla

Heads Up

I was playing keep-away when my friend Freddie threw the ball at me. It bonked me right on the head and bounced back to him! It looked like I'd done it on purpose, but I hadn't.

— Diana

Overboard!

My most embarrassing moment happened when I was eight years old. Six of my friends and I were swimming with floats. I suddenly fell out of the float and panicked. The water seemed really deep to me.

I started yelling, "I'm drowning! I'm drowning!"

My tallest friend helped me out of the water. I would have been okay anyway, because he told me that I had been in only three feet of water!

— Dakota

The Big Bounce

My birthday party was a swimming party, and I'd invited all of my friends. After everyone arrived, we wanted to go into the pool. We decided to get my little exercise trampoline and use it as a springboard into the pool. We set it on the side of the shallow end, right on the rim.

We all stood in line and pretended like it was a real diving board. One by one we jumped into the pool. When it was my turn, I stepped onto the trampoline, not noticing it was wet. I bounced a few times and was ready to jump in.

Instead, I slipped and *fell* into the pool. I was so embarrassed that my mom had to pull me out. My niece started laughing at me, and I felt so stupid that I laughed, too. Many days have passed and I still don't mess with that trampoline!

— Kendra

Celebrity Confession: Seth Rogen, who plays Ken on NBC's <u>Freaks and Geeks</u>

When I was a little kid, like ten years old, I used to pick my nose, and it caused a couple of embarrassing situations. I never ate it or anything; I would just manually clear blockages every once in a while. One time, in the second grade, everyone was eating lunch in the classroom, and we had a janitor watching us to make sure we didn't go nuts or anything.

So, I was sitting in the back corner of the room eating my lunch and I found I was having difficulty breathing through my nose. I looked around to make sure nobody was looking, and I dug in.

All of a sudden, I hear the janitor who was watching us say, "Ewwww! Seth picks his nose!"

Everyone burst out laughing and started to make fun of me.

Luckily, it didn't ruin my life or anything, because I'm sure everyone picks their nose once in a while. It's just a fact that not every nasal road-block is removable merely by blowing, and the bottom line is that everyone wants to breath easy.

I did learn something through this ordeal however. From that day forth, whenever I felt the urge to go "digging for gold" in school, I would ask to go to the bathroom and do it there.

Chapter Four

Dennis the Menace

If you saw the movie, then you know that Dennis was a kid who caused nothing but trouble for everyone around him. You may find that *your* "Dennis" comes in many shapes and forms. Sometimes he's a friend, sometimes he's an object, and sometimes he's a force of nature. Sometimes, he's just bad luck. Sometimes he's you!

The only thing you can be sure of is that whoever or whatever your personal "Menace" is, you're bound to be the one who gets embarrassed. Just like Mr. Wilson, you'll find yourself screaming "Arrgh!"

Open Sesame

One day when I was in the third grade, we had just finished all of our work in the classroom. It

33

was time to go for a bathroom break. My day had been going great until it happened.

My friends Hunter and Chantel opened the door to a rest room stall — while I was using it! They started laughing, and then they couldn't stop. I started to laugh, too, but felt mad and disgusted with them both.

When I went out, I could feel my cheeks turning red, and not just plain red, but dark red. My teacher told Hunter and Chantel to say they were sorry. She knew what had happened because people in class had told her.

By the time it was lunch, I overheard a boy named Dion talking about what had happened to me! Luckily, the lunchroom lady told him to stop.

— Roberta

The Longest Day Ever

One of my most embarrassing days happened when I was in the second grade. First, I was almost late for school, because I was trying to get my hair just right.

Then in my first class, I nearly tipped my desk over. I thought things couldn't get any worse but when I went to lunch, I dropped a whole plate of food. I couldn't believe it!

But it didn't stop. I got in trouble for blowing bubble gum in class. I couldn't wait to get home, but then when I went to bed I hit my head on the headboard. I woke up from my nap and decided to play on the swings. I fell and scratched my arm all up. Then I noticed my brothers spinning their bikes' wheels, and I went over to watch. Naturally, my leg got caught in one of the wheels and got pinched. I couldn't wait for the day to be over!

— Tara

Swan Lake

Last year when I was eight years old, I went to visit my grandparents. They have a pond where you can feed the ducks — and one swan.

My cousins were visiting my grandparents, too, and we were going to play by the pond, but one cousin was scared of the birds. Becca, Jade, my grandma, and I had lunch, and afterward my cousin wasn't scared anymore.

So we went down to feed the ducks and swan. But when we tried to feed the ducks, the mean swan would eat their food and bite them. So we fed the mean swan, too.

Suddenly, the swan jumped out of the pond and started chasing me. Becca and Jade were scared. I was scared, too, and everyone was watching me. The neighbors stepped out of their houses to see what was going on. Even people riding by on bikes stopped. Everyone was laughing at me.

I shouted, "Get away from me, shoo . . . shoo."

Finally, the swan bit me with his sharp teeth! Luckily, my leg only bled a little, but it hurt. I was so embarrassed. I felt like a baby for running away from the swan. I didn't want anyone to see me, but they all did.

— Autumn

Bust a Move

I would like to tell you about my friend Otto's very embarrassing moment.

It all started on a Saturday morning when I asked my dad if I could go to Otto's house. My dad said okay, and I walked next door. I knocked, and Otto's older sister, Maureen, answered.

She told me to come in, and we started watching TV. Suddenly, the bathroom door flew open and there was Otto dancing naked! I think he was doing the Macarena. Well, anyway, he saw me and ran back into the bathroom.

His sister and I burst out laughing. I'll never forget that day.

— Laura

Bad Hair Day

I was in the barbershop getting a last-minute haircut before I had to go to a wedding. There were thirty minutes left before I had to leave. The barber had just cut the hair on one side of my head when a major power failure happened. It lasted for an hour or so, and I couldn't wait around. I was so embarrassed looking at myself in the mirror with only one side of my hair cut! And I still had to go to the wedding like that.

— Skip

Strike a Pose

When I was nine years old, my parents and I were baby-sitting these kids, Amber, Emily, Lily, and Rosie.

When we went up to Lily's room, we found some wigs. And believe it or not, I look like a girl when I put a girl's wig on.

I went downstairs to show my parents. Emily decided that she would take pictures of me — she convinced me that it would be funny. She took a couple of me posing. I even put another wig on, and she took some more shots. We were all laughing and joking.

Later, I was embarrassed about the whole thing. I'd thought it would be hilarious to show the pictures at school, but I'd have been even more embarrassed if I'd done that. Now I know I won't ever wear a wig again!

— Edgar

Celebrity Confession: Jennifer Gillom, Team Captain and Center, WNBA Phoenix Mercury

My most embarrassing story happened one Sunday afternoon when I was about twelve years old. That week our church was filled with my relatives and other visitors from out of town. I got myself all dressed up and decided to top it off by wearing my mother's pantyhose. Even though they were obviously too big for me, I couldn't resist trying them on. To keep them in place, I slipped a pair of my own underwear over the pantyhose. It seemed like the perfect solution, and boy, did I look good.

I made it to church just fine, and didn't give it another thought until I found myself rocking and singing with the choir — and I felt something give! The elastic on my underwear had snapped and suddenly they were falling down. There was no way to stop their fall without people taking notice, so I let them slide down to my ankles.

I happened to be in the first row and was the first to walk back down the aisle when the service was over. Actually, I wasn't walking; it was more like shuffling. I was really humiliated at the time, but since then it has become one of the funniest stories that I share with my friends.

Chapter Five

Footloose

Kevin Bacon dances, leaps, rolls, and twists his way to happiness in the movie *Footloose*. No matter what he does he lands on his feet. But, let's face it, when the rest of us get "footloose," we end up losing our balance, our cool, our dignity, or worse!

Kneed Some Help?

When my uncle had a big graduation party, he invited all of his friends to my house. At the time, I was about eight years old. We had music, food, and everything to make him and his friends feel at home.

I got thirsty and went to the beverage table, because my orange soda was on it. I saw two stools sitting beside the table, and I climbed on one of them so that I could reach my drink. But I still couldn't grab it, so I knee-walked onto the next stool. I didn't watch where my knee was going and I fell off the stool onto the floor! Everyone looked at me, giggled a little, and then went back to talking and eating. Someone asked if I was okay, and I said I was.

I started skipping to my room, acting happy so people might think I fell on purpose. But once I got to my room, I wanted to die!

— Payton

You're Welcome

One day, my mom, my dad, my little brother, and I were shopping at the grocery store. It all happened because our household is very big on manners. Saying "please," "thank you," and "excuse me" are important.

We were messing around and talking, but we did buy a few things in the store. Then we paid for everything. On the way out, I was having a nice long conversation with my mom, and as I strolled through the open doors, I said thank you. That's when I realized that the doors were automatic and had opened by themselves!

Lots of people were watching, so I was very embarrassed.

— Finn

Got Your Goat

When I was in third grade, I went to a private school, which had its own farm with horses, goats, and other animals.

One windy day at recess, we were lining up when someone yelled, "Get that goat off the fence!"

One of the goats had climbed on top of the fence around the animal area.

I ran fast to get the goat down, but I forgot it was a windy day. I didn't realize that the wind was blowing my dress straight up. Everybody in my class started laughing! At first I didn't know why, but then some girl loudly told me what had happened. Everybody laughed even harder.

— Janie

Look Out Below!

Last year, I had to do a special project for school and decided to make a volcano. I was excited because I was going to make the volcano erupt. It would start to bubble and then shoot out foam.

I worked on it for three or four days before I was done with it. Afterward, I put it beside my bed. I was so proud of it.

But when I was fast asleep, I somehow rolled over and fell right on top of my project! I couldn't believe it, but I still had to bring it in to school because it was due that day.

I had to show up with a caved-in volcano.

— Baxter

Rocky Road

I was at school and we were eating lunch outside. I ran up to the teacher to get a straw and tripped over some rocks. I fell right in front of my friends. I got up and fell again! This time I'd sprained my ankle and I began to cry my lungs out. The teacher had to pick me up and carry me to the office. I started hollering louder and louder. They had to call my mom and dad to come and get me.

— Wiley

Excuse Me

One day, Fallon and I went to the mall to get Shonquelle's hair curled for the Valentine's dance. It was time to leave, and Fallon and I were racing each other to the mall doors. I won, of course.

People were walking through one door, so I ran right up to the other one. I didn't realize it was automatic, and it swung open and hit me. I wasn't injured. But the people passing by laughed — and so did Fallon.

— Sasha

Upside-down Cake

It was my mother's birthday and I was bringing in the cake. All the candles were lit, and everyone was ready to sing "Happy Birthday" — when I dropped the cake and ruined it!

— Joey

Ice with That?

One day, I was with my cousin at the supermarket. We started running around and acting crazy. Suddenly, we crashed against a "wall" of Coca-Cola cans. Imagine the huge mess all over the floor!

— Nicole

Birthday Bummer

It was fall, and it was my sixth birthday. My family had a turkey feast and a big, chocolate cake shaped like a turkey.

Afterward, I started yelling, "Hey, let's go buy my birthday present!"

I wanted to buy this cool toy I'd always wanted. I couldn't wait.

So we went to the mall, and my brother and I

started playing and running around. Then I got tired and stopped to tie my shoe. I was bending down when I heard a big ripping noise. My pants had split open. People were looking and laughing. I'd never felt so embarrassed in my life.

— Milo

Where's the Whipped Cream?

It was Halloween last year, and my dad told me that we were going to celebrate it at church. When we got there, I was excited to get some candy and wear a ghost costume.

While my brother played Nintendo, I was trading Pokémon cards with friends.

My mom came in and said, "It's time for dinner, and we're having pumpkin pie for dessert."

Everyone was sitting in the main dining room.

I wasn't hungry, and I don't like pumpkin pie, so I decided to run into the kitchen and hide. But I fell and crashed into the table where the pie was! I had pumpkin pie all over my face.

— Larry

Too Slick

It was winter, and there was a lot of snow on the ground. The first thing I did at school was have breakfast in the cafeteria with my friend Neil. Afterward, I decided to go outside. It just so happened that there were a lot of older kids around, fifth and sixth graders. I noticed the snow all over as I opened the door. But it didn't look that bad, so I jumped down the first step. Then I landed on a huge ice patch and slipped! When I fell, I landed on my back, and my butt hit the ice hard. Everyone turned around and looked at me — then they laughed.

— Ron

Too Big for Your Britches

One day, Mom asked me to go shopping for clothes. I told her that I didn't want to, because a cartoon show was coming on and it only showed once. My mom made me go anyway.

Once we were in the car, my mom asked, "Why don't you really want to go? Tell me the truth."

I finally told her I was afraid that my friend Darrin, who was mad at me, would be there. We got to the mall, and I found some pants to try on. Holding the pants up, I left the dressing room to show my mom. She told me they were too big. So I ran back to the dressing room and, on the way, I fell. When I got up, the pants had fallen, too — all the way down, and my underwear was showing!

Just then, Darrin walked by. He saw the whole thing! I didn't want to leave my house for the entire weekend.

— George

Alley Oops

When I was in Colorado, I went bowling with my grandma and siblings. I was in last place as always. Everyone else had tons of points. But I didn't mind. I thought everything was going fine.

But then it was my turn. I swung the ball forward, but I couldn't let go. My arm went backward instead, and the ball went flying behind me. It landed in the snack bar and lounge area! I almost hit a stranger, and the ball made an awful noise when it landed. The whole bowling alley

saw; everyone was staring at me. I was so humiliated.

Since then I have learned to keep a very tight
grip on a bowling ball!

— Dinah

Celebrity Confession: Tangi Miller, who plays Elena in WB's <u>Felicity</u>

We were doing a group scene in a restaurant
setting. Scott Foley (Noel), Amy Jo Johnson
(Julie), and I were already sitting down when Keri
Russell (Felicity) and Scott Speedman (Ben)
strolled in. This was a very big moment because
Felicity had just chosen Ben over Noel. This was
around the same time Felicity had cut her hair.

In the scene, Noel and Ben started getting into
it, and I (as Elena) told them to cut it out. At that
moment, the scene was stopped and we all took a
break. The chairs and tables we were using were
removed and would be brought back later.

When we returned to restart the scene, we all
went back to our original places. But when I went
to sit down, I flew with a bang to the floor! They'd
forgotten to replace my chair. Everyone was in

shock because they hadn't realized what had happened. The prop guy understood the situation, though, and rushed over to help me up. But when I tried to rise, my head was jerked back, because he was stepping on my braids!

Keri started screaming loudly, thinking something was really wrong. Everyone thought I was hurt. It wasn't until I was finally able to get up and tell them that I was okay that they all started laughing.

In a restaurant scene, you have a lot of people around, which made it all the more embarrassing. I'm still trying to live down that incident.

Cheryl Miller, Head Coach, WNBA Phoenix Mercury

Well, my story is about me and my brother, Reggie (who plays for the Indiana Pacers). Growing up, we always played pranks on each other.

When we were in junior high and elementary school, our parents always had to double-check and make sure we were up for school. Both Reggie and I loved to sleep in, so every minute counted. No matter what time we set the alarm for, we always managed to be running late. And it never failed that Reggie would blame me for our tardiness.

This one morning, thanks to Reggie's messing around, we got to school twenty minutes late. Not only was our teacher upset, but we had to give speeches that day, and she made me go first. Yuck! I was so nervous. Then I had to stay after school for one hour while Reggie went on his merry way home! Well, I had every intention of getting him back. My wheels started spinning. . . .

Although it took me two days, I got him good. I waited until he left his bedroom, then went in and changed the time on his alarm clock. The alarm went off in the middle of the night, and Reggie thought it was morning. He jumped in the shower and started getting ready for school. The sound of running water woke my whole family up. My dad told Reggie to get out of the shower because it was the middle of night.

Well, Reggie realized he'd been had, and he wasn't laughing. I was lying in my cozy bed chuckling. I got the last laugh that time.

Chapter Six

The Parent Trap

It was so cute when those adorable twins tried to get their parents back together. The girls resorted to all sorts of tricks and pranks and, of course, they succeeded in "trapping" their parents.

But the real deal is that it's usually the kids who end up trapped in their parents' crazy messes! They may not do it on purpose, but moms and dads always seem to be causing some major embarrassment for their offspring.

Wiped Out

That day, I had a baseball game and reminded my mom to get my uniform ready. I couldn't wait to play, and kept thinking about whether we were going to win or lose.

When I got to the field, my coach yelled for us to do warm-ups. So, we all started doing our exercises.

A few minutes later, my mom walked out onto the field and said to me, "Tom, you can't play with a dirty face."

She pulled out — okay, are you ready for this — a baby wipe! And proceeded to clean my face with it.

I shouted, "Mom!" I felt like the whole world was against me.

Luckily, she never did that again.

— Tom

Food Fight

My family and I went to a restaurant after we visited a nearby park. We ordered our dinners first, and then my mom and I went up to the salad bar. I told her what I wanted. She was putting broccoli on my plate when I accidentally pulled on her arm. She spilled the entire plate on me! I was covered with all kinds of food.

— Vincent

Picture This

One day, I had my friends Sharon and Lani over. We played basketball games, then my mom called for us all to come inside. She said she wanted to show us something.

She happened to be looking through all my baby pictures. She showed them to my friends. I was so embarrassed.

I wanted to stop her so I asked if dinner was ready. At least while we were eating she couldn't show those pictures! But she said it wasn't quite ready and showed more baby pictures.

My friends were saying things like "How cute!" and "What a doll!"

— Becky

Lost in Space

One day my mom rearranged my furniture without telling me. I was too tired to notice before I went to bed. But when I woke up in the middle of the night to go to the bathroom, I felt as if I was in some strange place. I started crying and shouting out loud for help.

I woke up my little sister, and she started crying out loud, too. Then I turned on the light and saw that I was in my own room — but my furniture had been moved around.

— Shawn

A Tight Fit

One day, I went to play at my friend's house. We were having a lot of fun when my mom suddenly showed up. She said she came to check on me because the shorts I was wearing were way too small. She thought I might tear them or something. My friends started laughing.

— Skye

Rapunzel

Once my hair was very long. Then my mom decided to give me a haircut. Let me tell you that I don't like it when my mom brings out the scissors!

I didn't want my hair to be too short. But I sat down and let my mom start cutting. I was hoping she was listening to me when I told her how I wanted my hair to be.

But when I looked at myself in the mirror, I almost had no hair at all! And I had to go to school like that, too.

— Tatiana

Celebrity Confession: Cherie Bennett, author, <u>Searching for David's Heart</u> (Delacorte, 1998), <u>Anne Frank & Me</u> (Dramatic Publishing Co., 1997), nationally syndicated columnist, "Hey, Cherie" (Copley News Service)

When I was twelve, I was thrilled when I was cast in a musical at the local dinner theater. The cast was mostly adult professional actors, and I was beyond intimidated. My costume consisted of a yellow lacy dress with a full skirt, petticoats, and the world's ugliest matching frilly yellow panties.

When I did my dance number, the dress was supposed to fly up and expose those frilly panties, and it did. Underneath them, I wore a nude-colored leotard, but from the audience, you couldn't tell I had anything else on.

One night, midway through my big dance number, the elastic broke on the panties. There I was, center stage, and those yellow panties had fallen off in front of four hundred people. What could I do? I just kept dancing. So, everyone in the cast is dancing around these panties, laughing so hard that they're actually crying.

When I got to the center stage again, I kicked the panties into the orchestra pit where they landed on the guitarist's head. And I had the world's biggest crush on this guy.

You'll notice I ended up becoming a writer instead of an actress. No one knows *what* I'm wearing, and no one cares. I do not, however, own any yellow underwear.

Wendy Palmer, Forward, WNBA Detroit Shock

My most embarrassing moment occurred when I was in the eighth grade. I was by far the most athletic girl in school, which drew a lot of attention. Like all young girls, I had a crush on the most popular boy in school. On this particular day, he just happened to be standing in the doorway watching volleyball practice.

The volleyball coach, Sandra Matthews, was and still is one of the most influential people in my life. And Mrs. Matthews is a practical joker. Earlier in practice, she had gotten on us for not properly lowering our bodies for jumping. So, she made one final warning, and I was listening. However, she wasn't satisfied with my performance.

Now, I was in the front line preparing to block. Mrs. Matthews took it upon herself to pull my pants down! Neither she nor my teammates knew that on that particular day I'd run out of underwear and had thrown on my mom's prized possession — her favorite underpants, which seemed to swallow my six-foot, 130-pound frame. As I began to leap in the air, my shorts fell down to my ankles. I froze in embarrassment, then fell to the ground, holding my face. Everyone burst out laughing, including the cutest guy in school.

Well, it didn't work out so badly. He began to speak to me, even after he got a look at my underwear!

Chapter Seven

The Addams Family

In the last chapter, we discussed how parents can drive us crazy, but lots of times, it's our other family members who make us want to hide. You don't even need monsters and ghouls in your home to make it a dangerously embarrassing place. Your own siblings can do that for you.

Don't Tread on Me

One day, my brother asked me if I wanted to go to work with him. I said okay, so we went to his office. We were taking a break, and my brother asked if I'd like to run on the treadmill. I thought about it and said sure.

I got on the treadmill and started running in place. Then, I jumped off, and my brother climbed on. He turned the speed up, but then turned it back down when he got off. It was my turn again, and I was going at my own pace when my brother decided to increase the speed. This time, he turned it *all* the way up. It was going superfast and I couldn't keep up. Suddenly, my legs gave out and I skidded off the treadmill. I skinned my left elbow. My brother laughed so hard that he started to cry. He also told all of his friends about it.

— Greg

Walk This Way

One day, my big sister, Nora, her friends Tracy and Tyra, and I were all walking home. It was evening, and Nora was telling a story. I wanted to hear it and see what was going on, so I started to walk backward.

But then, Nora started walking faster, so I was forced to walk backward faster. Her friend sped up, too.

Tracy and Tyra said, "You're going to fall."

I said, "Yeah, right. I'm not that dumb."

I could tell they didn't believe me. We continued walking, and I tripped and fell backward!

Naturally, Nora and her friends started laughing. I just got up and continued walking backward.

Tyra said, "Watch, you're going to run into a pole."

I told her I wouldn't. But, right then, I bumped into a pole. Of course!

— Brianna

Hard Day's Work

One summer, my cousins Robby and Dave and I were in my dad's workshop. We were putting sodas in the Coke machine, and decided it was time to take a break. It was hot, and we decided to go outside and drink some Cokes. I sat down and after a little while I felt something on my legs and back. It felt like something was biting me.

Then, my cousins started laughing because I was dancing around like crazy. I realized I had sat on an anthill.

We went back to work, even though the bites were making me feel bad. Then I accidentally dropped a can of soda and sprayed it all over the middle of my pants. My cousins thought I'd wet my pants. They were laughing really hard and then they decided to drop their cans of soda so I got sprayed all over!

It didn't end there. Some stray dog wandered in and licked me from head to toe!

— Andy

Uncovered

Two years ago, we had Thanksgiving at my house, and the whole family was there. I was upstairs watching TV when my little cousin Aidan came up to play with me. I left the room for one moment and when I came back I saw that Aidan had gotten into my dresser. He had opened my underwear drawer!

I ran downstairs, but it was too late. Aidan was marching through the house, swinging my underpants around. I ran to my room and didn't come out till the next day.

— Bree

Time Out!

One day, I was playing football with my uncle Simon. He threw the ball to me, and I took off running after it. I was so excited. But as soon as I caught it, I slammed right into a pole! I wasn't injured, though my head did hurt.

— Virgil

In the Bag

Last year, I went camping in Maine. It was a great day, and everyone was getting ready to sleep. My little sister had already gone to bed. I thought she was in her sleeping bag, though I couldn't see her.

I climbed into my own sleeping bag and started screaming. She started screaming, too. My little sister was deep inside my bag. She had scared me really bad. Everyone woke up and started yelling, too. I'd scared them. I was so mad at my little sister.

— Connor

Celebrity Confession: Michelle Krusiec, who plays Sui, on NBC's <u>One World</u>

I was always very conscious of my clothes growing up, because our family didn't have a lot of money, and I always wore my brothers' hand-me-downs. One particular summer (I was going into the seventh grade), my mother went to Taiwan to visit our relatives and returned with a lot of Taiwanese clothing. As regards the clothes, let's just say this — she could have left the fashion in Taiwan.

She brought back sandals with these big, thick heels and pants that were cut off at the knee with prints sewn onto the bottom.

Well, I wore them to school with my mother encouragingly shouting at me, "New style, new American style!" as I made my way to the bus stop.

I didn't want to hurt her feelings, but I knew everyone would be interrogating me about my new clothes. Of course, they did, because the clothes were so unusual. I was embarrassed, but I was more terrified that the clothes made me look so different.

But now I realize that style isn't about clothing, it's about one's confidence.

Chapter Eight

Fame

In the old movie *Fame*, kids dance, sing, and do just about anything to become famous. They love being noticed and love having an audience watch them. Some people really shine when they're on center stage. And, then, there's the rest of us.

Being in the spotlight can be a thrill — or not. Somehow, when all eyes are on us, we tend to turn into klutzes, and our big moments turn into big comedy acts, whether we want them to or not.

Fame can so easily turn into infamy!

Rah-rah!

I was asked to participate in the third-grade talent show, along with many other people. It took me a while to respond, but then I said yes. I went as a cheerleader from our high school. I borrowed a costume from my neighbor, and she helped me with my routine.

Finally, it was the day of the talent show, and I had to give my cheer. I began with two double cartwheels, and then I shouted the words. The room was really small, and the entire third grade was watching me. I started doing cartwheels again — and suddenly I lost control. I crashed right into some cubby doors! My pom-poms flew in the air.

But I got back up and finished the routine. Later, I told them all it was a comedy act.

— Magda

Kung Fu Fighting

It was time for my first Tae Kwon Do lesson, and I was so nervous. I didn't know anything about karate. My brother was going to class with me, but he didn't seem nervous at all. My mom dropped us off and wished us good luck.

I walked into the room, and saw kids stretching, kicking, and punching. The teacher came over to my brother and me and told us his name was Master Li. We introduced ourselves, too.

Then the class began. Master Li told us to get partners. My brother got one quickly, but I just stood there for a while. Finally, some girl came over and asked if I wanted to be her partner. Naturally, I said yes.

She stood and held her hand out. I was supposed to kick her hand gently, then aim a punch lightly at her hand. First I tried kicking and missed completely. Then, I tried a punch and missed again! I heard people laughing. Then I realized that they were laughing at *me*.

I felt like such a baby and a loser.

— Ella

Music to My Ears

Our church has a children's program, and we were putting on a Christmas musical. I had a solo part in it, and I was scared. My face was red, and I was shaky.

I don't do well in front of large audiences. A boy named Geno also had a solo. He was performing first, and I was worrying the whole time that I didn't know my song that well.

I kept thinking, *What if I mess up? What will happen?*

Finally, the music started, and it was time for me to go on. I sang the first line correctly, but then I got super-nervous and forgot the next line. Oh, no! My youth pastor started helping me out. I remembered the next line and started singing again. I was so thankful.

But, then, for some reason, my voice went up really high, and it squeaked! It wasn't supposed to do that.

— Penny

Wedding March

It was Thanksgiving and it was my sister's wedding day. I had been chosen to be the bridesmaid, one of the most important people in the wedding! I had to walk down the aisle with the best man. I was wearing a very long dress, and a pair of really high, high, white sandals. They must have had five-inch heels! I felt like such a grown-up marching down the aisle, but then suddenly I tripped over my dress, twisted my ankle, and fell over *right* when everybody was taking a picture of me!

Everyone laughed, including the bride and groom. I stood up and twisted my ankle again. I finally got my balance and started walking very fast until the best man pulled me back and made me walk a little slower.

— Wren

Butterfingers

Last year, my friends and I were going to play chimes in our church. After young people's time was over, it would be our turn to perform.

Before I went on, my mom said, "I hope you do well."

"Me, too," I said.

Then it was time. The first song was great, but then when it was time for the second song, I had switched the chimes around in my hand. I had them backward and played the wrong chimes!

My parents tried telling me how well I did, but I knew I'd made a mistake.

— Cooper

Stage Nightmare

In the second grade, we were going to put on a program for the PTA. My teacher pleaded with us to be on time for opening night.

I got ready and studied my lines. I thought to myself, *Tonight, I'm going to be the* bomb.

It was six o'clock and time for our show to begin. My mom, sister, and brother were sitting in the audience. I peeked through the curtains and saw a huge crowd. We all got a big lecture about not forgetting our lines. We were supposed to be giving speeches about the Ark. While our teacher was talking to us, I didn't really pay attention. I was confident that I was going to do a great job.

One by one, everyone gave their speeches. No one messed up.

Then it was my turn. As I walked to the middle of the stage, I didn't see the long, black wire stretched across the floor. Boom! I hit the floor facefirst. I got up and felt my face. It was covered with dirt. I just stood there and looked at the audience.

I was only able to say, "Uh, uh, uh."

Finally, my friend, who was behind the curtain, whispered my whole speech to me.

Afterward, everyone came out and bowed. As the curtain was falling down, I was still bowing, and it fell right on me! It took three people to pull me out.

— Carrie

Ring-Around-the-Rosy

When I was four, I was a ring bearer at my aunt's wedding. It was summer, and my family and aunt's friends were all going to be there. My mom told me that my job was the most important one at the wedding.

The wedding began. I was afraid that I would lose the wedding rings, but I was doing just fine at first, looking straight ahead. I didn't even look at the pillow I was carrying. Then, I turned around and mouthed something at my mom. When I turned back around, I finally looked down. The wedding rings were gone! I didn't say a word, but I started to cry.

The wedding went on anyway. Afterward, my mom told me that they had taken the rings off the pillow before the ceremony. I was so glad that I hadn't lost them. But I was so embarrassed because I had cried in front of everyone and no one knew why.

— Jackson

Look at Me!

I was really excited when I started to ride my bike. My sister was trying to teach me some tricks. They were really fun to do. It was hard work, but I was a quick learner. I was so happy to be on the open road.

My whole family was watching, and I couldn't wait to show them how I could ride my bike. I also decided to practice some of my tricks at the same time. I stood up and took away one hand. Then I crashed and hurt my knees. My family started laughing. No one realized I was in pain until I started crying. My knees were bleeding. From then on, I wouldn't do any more tricks. And I still don't think it was funny!

— Sloan

Chapter Nine

Scream

In this famous movie, some really scary guy chased the characters around, making them scream in horror. But you don't need a creep in a mask to make you want to disappear.

And, as you may know personally, some things are so embarrassing and so humiliating that even screaming isn't enough. The following stories will make it all clear!

Twist and Shout

One Saturday afternoon, I went to my girlfriend Kess's birthday party. My cousin Bennett was there, along with my friend Shawn. We played spin the bottle and other party games. Then we played a game of Twister. I was going up against Kess.

She's in gymnastics and was warming up. We were going to play the ultimate game! I started on a red circle. A few seconds later, they called another color, and I was bending over with my butt in Kess's face.

I was trying to hold it in, but I just couldn't. I passed gas, really loud. I ran out of that house as fast I could. It was so embarrassing that we broke up.

— Thom

Calling All Nerds

I went to my best friend Ramon's house to play video games and shoot some hoops. Then we went bike riding. When we got back, we went to Ramon's sister's room. We started spraying perfume around just for fun. Then we started eating Nerds candy. I ate three boxes. I was bouncing off the walls.

Suddenly, after eating all of that candy and smelling so much perfume, I felt like I couldn't breathe. The room seemed to be spinning around.

I started laughing but that only made it worse. I threw up all over. Nerds and orange juice exploded from my nose and mouth.

Ramon's sister came into her room and started screaming. She called for their mom.

Ramon was laughing, but I was thinking, *Oh, man!*

His mom came up and said, "Ramon, you're going to have to clean this all up."

No more Nerds and perfume for me!

— Noel

Bottoms Up

One time when I was four, my mom and I decided to go to the beach. I was wearing a two-piece swimsuit, and I'd gotten sand in the bottoms. It was so uncomfortable! My mom told me to go wash the sand out in the ocean.

I walked out so deep that I couldn't reach the bottom. I started kicking my legs so that I could keep my head above the water. That was difficult because I wasn't a great swimmer. I was ready to get the sand out of my suit.

Then suddenly I noticed that the bottom of my

two-piece had fallen off! I looked all around but couldn't find it anywhere! I had to yell to Mom to bring me a towel. I had to get out of the water wrapped in it. I never did find the rest of my swimsuit.

— Lynn

Accidents Will Happen

When I was in the first grade, it was time for gym class. I happened to be wearing this really pretty dress. We were just supposed to change into sneakers, and I was trying to unbuckle my shoes. Suddenly, I realized that I had to use the toilet — right away. I ran for the bathroom. My teacher was yelling at me to hurry up. I rushed but didn't make it, and ended up wetting all over the bathroom floor. All of the kids laughed at me.

I had to go home and change into a plain old T-shirt and shorts.

— Marley

Show Time!

In second grade, I brought a video of a popular movie that I thought all the kids would want to see. Everyone was eagerly waiting, so my teacher started the movie.

But instead of the cool movie, it was a tape my dad had made the night before of my sister and me dancing, singing, and doing cartwheels. I'd brought it by mistake, and the entire class was watching! Ever since then, I check each tape before I take it anywhere.

— Logan

Blown Away

We were on our way into town, when my mom decided to stop at Pizza Hut. My mom's friend's brother, who's in the tenth grade, said something really funny. All of us started laughing. I was cracking up so hard that gross stuff came out of my nose. Everyone noticed. They were all pointing at me!

— Zoe

Run Away

My sister and I were sick. My mom had given us some medicine that made us both have to use the bathroom a lot. My sister and I were getting bored sitting around the house, and we couldn't think of anything to do. That morning all we did was watch TV and argue for fun.

I got sick of watching talk shows, which is all my sister wanted to see. I decided to read my book and reached down for it. Just then, the medicine started to work, and I had the runs right then and there. I couldn't help it, and it went all over the floor!

— Scott

Caught by Surprise

It was a hot summer day, and I was at my house. My parents were in the living room with a visitor, some lady named Maureen. I was five or six at the time. Later, Maureen left to go for a walk, but I thought she had gone for good.

I decided to go out in the living room, and

since it was hot, I was wearing just my underwear. I was sitting in a nice, cold chair when Maureen suddenly walked back into our house! I was so surprised. Worse, she thought I looked cute and took my picture!

I felt so embarrassed that someone who wasn't a family member, especially an old lady who liked me, saw me in my underwear!

— Sabrina

Put a Lid on It!

My parents took me to visit some people I had never met before. I asked permission to use the bathroom. Afterward, I noticed that I hadn't lifted the toilet lid up! I wished I could vanish.

— Willow

Falling Down

It all started when I was sitting in class and decided I had to use the rest room. Afterward, I came back to class. We were working on math, and the teacher asked me to do a problem on the chalkboard. As I was walking up to the board, my pants fell to the floor. I'd forgotten to buckle them in the bathroom! I had to pull my pants up and buckle my belt in front of everyone.

— Glenn

Doesn't Add Up

This happened when I was in the fourth grade. I was in math class and my friend Molly was making funny faces at me. The teacher, who was up at the blackboard, turned around to look at me, and I tried to act like I wasn't laughing — but I was. Afterward, the teacher faced the blackboard again. I started laughing so hard again that I accidentally let one out. Molly heard me and lost it. Which made me laugh so hard again that I did it three more times! I was so embarrassed. I tried to act like I hadn't done anything, but Molly wouldn't stop laughing.

— Fawn

Somebody Help Me!

My friend Wesley and I went to the rodeo. I had to go to the bathroom, but once I got inside the stall, I realized that there wasn't any toilet paper. I didn't know what to do. It seemed like I was in there for hours.

Finally, Wesley came in and asked me, "What's taking you so long?"

I told him what the problem was.

He said, "I'll get you some."

Then he came back with empty popcorn bags! He *said* that was all he could find. Finally, some girl from school gave him some toilet paper. But instead of handing it to me, he threw it in a puddle on the floor. I had to use it anyway!

— Rik

Celebrity Confession: Lisa Harrison, Forward, WNBA Phoenix Mercury

I would have to say the funniest thing that stands out in my memory is what happened in 1992, while I was in college. It was my sophomore year at the University of Tennessee. Our basketball team, the "Lady Vols," was having a great season, and we were headed to The Women's Final Four in New Orleans. We made it to the championship game after beating Stanford in the semifinals. After a tough, physical game against Virginia in the finals, we won in overtime! We were the national champs!

After the game, we went back to the hotel to change and get ready to celebrate our victory. We went out with our teammates and fans and headed for Bourbon Street. Later when we returned to our room around midnight, Marlene and I discovered that someone had been there! We had been robbed. It was clear to us that our belongings had been disturbed, and our beds had been ruffled. We were scared to say the least.

We ran to our coaches' room to tell them what had happened. How could something like this happen in a first-class, top-rated hotel?

Our coaches came back with us to check things out.

Well, it was clear to our coaches what had happened. (Naturally, because they were used to the finer things in life.) We hadn't been robbed; the maids simply had come in while we were gone to turn down our beds! Boy, did we feel stupid. I guess it's true. You live and you learn.

Chapter 10

The End (Maybe)

Okay, we made it through another bunch of the most stomach-churning stories ever. How could so many embarrassing things happen to so many cool people? After reading them all, I feel like someone deserves a reward or prize. Us for getting through the book without collapsing in horror. And the authors of the stories, who not only lived to tell what happened to them, but also had the courage and confidence to share it all.

I was going to say that this really is the end. But knowing you guys, somehow I doubt it!